LOVE DOGS…

A Novel Story

By

Lori Hamilton

Gotham Books

30 N Gould St.
Ste. 20820, Sheridan, WY 82801
https://gothambooksinc.com/

Phone: 1 (307) 464-7800

Published by Gotham Books (November 22, 2023)

ISBN: 979-8-88775-578-6 (P)
ISBN: 979-8-88775-579-3 (E)

Table of Contents

CHAPTER ONE

Highway Dog-napping starring JimBob,
A Coonhound

JimBob was a magician. He could do the most unbelievable things. In fact, as I begin to tell you about them, I can't be sure you'll believe me. He was a true renegade, a gypsy, a clever, consummate thief, and powerful. He was a Tennessee Black and Tan Coonhound. I rescued him from the 23 Freeway near Fillmore, California, just as he was staggering across a narrow bridge. Fearing that oncoming traffic would hit him, I swung my car across both lanes, stopping any traffic while I would coax him into the car. He needed no coaxing, but jumped in back with two of my colleagues, neither of whom particularly liked dogs, especially big, funny looking dogs with very long ears.

The first car to come along was a sheriff. The Deputy explained that coonhounds were used for hunting in the Fillmore area. He theorized that JimBob had been out hunting when the recent big fires started and he was separated from his owners, leaving him to fend for himself.

He looked like he was starving so I drove to the nearest Big Mac and got three one pounders for him and a big cup of water. The water came first as he tanked up and then inhaled the burgers, looking at me for more. Now what to do with him? Well, I did what I always do when I find a stray dog: I take them home. I have actually been accused of dog-napping and on some occasions have probably been guilty. Now the big question was: How would Petite Chou, my adorable eight-pound toy poodle take to him? And how would he take to her?

Most hunters usually keep their dogs in the barn or a kennel. But if JimBob was kept in a barn, that barn had a sofa because he walked into our house and immediately jumped on the sofa, a good spot for surveying his new domain. For Petite Chou, it was love at first sight while he regarded her as a little insignificant sister. At every opportunity, she would stand beneath him and gaze adoringly at his underside. One could only guess at what she was thinking, or wishfully thinking. Life with coonhound was progressing peacefully until we heard this loud, weird sound ---ooouuuuuahhhh! Oooouuuuahhhh! Spooky! Our first introduction to a coonhound's baying was provoked by the invasion of a squirrel in the yard. From then on we were repeatedly treated to this special song and although initially it caused goosebumps, we eventually became very fond of it. Our guests were entertained, if surprised, in the middle of a party to suddenly be treated to the coonhound's baying performance.

We next learned that he didn't have any manners. I put two New York steaks in the broiler when the doorbell rang. When I came back, the steaks were gone. Another time, a big butterflied lamb was removed from the grill and set on the table to cool. Suddenly one of the guests said, "What does JimBob have?" as he was pawing at something on the ground. It was our roast! After stealthily stealing it from the table, he found it too hot to eat, so cleverly was rolling it around in the dirt to cool. Immediately, I saw myself running out to the market to get something for our guests to eat. But Jack rushed in, retrieved the roast and after a thorough rinsing, we were able to salvage it and serve our guests. They were good sports about it. Then we learned he was an escape artist. Our yard was totally fenced, but frequently I would look out my office window and see JimBob following the kids to school in the morning.

He loved going to school with them. Many times, the school would call me to come and get JimBob. "JimBob is here again." Once he went right inside the school. They caught him and locked him up in a closet. Chastized, even humiliated, there were no escapes this time.

Usually he returned by himself but one time he didn't come home. We combed the neighborhood. This was a challenge because you could see him one moment, and the next he would disappear into thin air. Finally, I called the shelter and they confirmed they had him. Walking past the cages, I passed right by my dog, not recognizing him. The dogs in shelters are so traumatized that not only their personalities change, but their features. He must have been in shock because he did not recognize me, either. On the drive home, happy to have him back, I started whistling. He stared at me, now recognizing me, leaned right in front of my face and gave me a big lick. A great big slurp up my face. You have no idea what a biggie this was. Coonhounds aren't known to be kissy-poos.

JimBob Coonhound with his favorite ball

My bed had a view of a large apricot tree in the back yard. One day I watched JimBob crawl up onto the lower branch and gingerly step forward on it, finally reaching the wooden fence. He climbed onto the narrow ledge, then walked it like a tightrope until he jumped down on the other side. Aha! Now I knew how he escaped. I ran next door to see him pushing the neighbor's gate open. He was most surprised to see me. One time, he was not so lucky. My neighbor related how she, too, saw him do his balancing act on the narrow ledge and then he fell off, with one leg caught between the pickets. She ran to call Animal Control for help and when she got back, Jim Bob was gone. He had miraculously managed to get that leg out while dangling upside down. The branch was cut down but some how he continued his incredible escapes. It only took a second for the door to be open, unguarded, and he was gone.

It's funny how dogs will take an intense dislike to another dog, while getting along with all the others. Some mornings, on the way to work, I would see a big spotted yellow dog. I knew he didn't belong to anyone in our neighborhood. I called him the Yellow Hyena dog. JimBob always knew when that dog had been around. On his evening walk, he would sniff, track, pull and bay, but only on the days Yellow Hyena dog had visited our street. By this time he was up to 85 pounds, so there was little argument when he decided to take off. The choices are to be pulled over or to let go of the leash. After skinning both knees, I learned to let go. Jack, at 220 pounds, tried holding him back and he, too, was pulled over. He was plenty mad about it. But not as mad as when he picked JimBob up for some now forgotten reason and JimBob tried biting his head. I remember making a joke about biting the head that feeds it. It didn't go over that well. Anyway, I'm glad we never had an encounter with Yellow Hyena dog. In the south, coonhounds are referred to as "cat" dogs. "Cat" as in mountain lion. There is a statue somewhere down there of a coonhound and a mountain lion depicted in the death of both of them, fighting to the end. I've heard from others who noticed their dog had a particular dislike of one dog. Our good friends, the Davis's, had a beautiful Collie, Bruce, who hated the dog across the street. Even if Hobo went by in a car, Bruce wanted to attack. The Davis's had another dog, little Buster Brown. We wanted to introduce Buster to JimBob, thinking they would naturally be friends, too. But when they arrived at our house with Buster, JimBob took one look and went wild, ready to attack. We put JimBob outside, brought Buster inside, hoping JimBob would calm down. An hour later, he was still banging at the sliding glass doors, ferociously trying to get at Buster. We gave up and the Davis's took Buster and went home, understanding dog psychology as only dog-owners can.

JimBob Coonhound reluctantly submits to a hug

You could say that JimBob was housebroken, in a way. We used a can of pennies to throw at him if we could catch him in the act of lifting his leg on furniture. There were frequent signs that we were totally unsuccessful. For some time there had been a bad smell in the living room. I searched carefully many times and could not find the source until I decided to replant a potted fern and there it was. He had backed up to the only acceptable spot in the house, a green plant, like a good dog.

JimBob looks contrite by The Potted palm.

JimBob was certainly lovable but also untrainable. "Come" was an abstraction, or it possibly meant "go" or "keep going" because that's what he did when called. Walking him in a rugged arroyo near our house was exercise for my lungs. He would suddenly take off, I'd spot him off in the distance, and start calling, calling, calling which he totally ignored. The tracking of a deer, or a rabbit was just too important to him. One Sunday morning, waking at 6 am, I decided to walk both Petite Chou and JimBob down to the arroyo. It was a challenge for Petite Chou, because now at 16, and nearly blind, she would bump into twigs or rocks on the path. The three of us were leisurely strolling when a coyote suddenly emerged from a large clump of bushes ahead and then disappeared. JimBob ran into the bushes after it. Fearing it was a female luring him into a pack, I snatched up Petite Chou and went after him. He was so busy with the tantalizing scent, I was able to catch him and drag him out. Frightened out of my wits by now, we ran the five blocks home. Breathlessly, I related the story to Jack. He leaned back in bed and said "Uhhuh". He didn't believe me. He always said I had a terrific imagination, but this was real. On numerous occasions, when I retold the story, he would wink and do his 'Uhh-huh" routine, totally discrediting me. It was infuriating. But there would be payback. On one of his walks, he, too, encountered a coyote and that was the end of the "Uhhhhuhh's" when I told my stories. 'Although our streets are littered with signs and pictures of "missing" dogs, the rewards offered for their return largely go uncollected. There is little doubt about their fate, especially the smaller dogs. But we believe in co-existing with wildlife. They do us a service in keeping other wild life in check. Our neighborhood has an ever - increasing population of rabbits in spite of occasionally finding partially digested bunny parts on the front lawn. Bunnies are cute but I liked them more before one got in our garden. For twenty years I had been trying to grow Chinese Lanterns. I got one up to a height of six inches, thrilled with this hard-won success.

When it disappeared without a trace, the finger could only be pointed at that "cute" intruder. Anyway, our well-fed coyotes have full, beautiful coats and are quite secure strolling down the street in daylight. In fact, one strolled past my neighbor who was walking with her Yorkie. The Yorkie took off after the coyote who ran, then stopped and turned around to see who was chasing him. You could almost hear the claws on the street as the Yorkie put on her brakes, stopping a respectable distance from the coyote who. with a contemptuous toss of its head, turned and sauntered off. If our small dogs and cats weren't so threatened by their presence, we probably would be proud of our coyotes.

CHAPTER TWO

JimBob Flirts with Danger,
Introducing Cleopattera

Not to be outdone by my found treasure (JimBob, of course), Jack checked the classified ads in the local newspaper. There it was: "a sweet, small, well-behaved female terrier mix desperately needs a new home." It was a surprise to discover that home would be ours. When asked to describe this scruffy new dog, Jack would say, "She's grey, black, brown, white, blue and some red." I could tell you her front legs seemed shorter and kind of crooked, her body overly long, her fur both short and long. Let's just say she'd never make it in a dog show. It was terrible the way people would ask, "What is it?" I'd respond, "She's a Terr-ee-AY." French, you know. To give her a little panache, I named her Cleopattera.

But it was love at first sight for JimBob. Or at first scent, because it was our bad luck that the moment she entered our home, she came into season. We kept her in the bedroom with us at night and JimBob in the other section of the house. When I got up that morning, I found Cleopattera huddled behind the toilet in the guest bathroom, trembling with fear as JimBob tried to get at her. Then we saw the door that led to the bedroom wing. Demolished! JimBob had chewed right through a sturdy two-inch oak door. That more or less gave the signal that it was time for him to be neutered.

Cleopattera, as small as she was, wanted to be dominant and lead. On our walks, juggling three dogs of graduated sizes, she insisted on pulling out in front. She managed somehow to keep several steps ahead of JimBob, no mean feat. She quickly learned JimBob's escape trick, and if he was fast before, he couldn't keep up with TerreeAy so she led the way, and he followed. The problem was that he had a homing

11

instinct and she didn't. So their forays went further and further and eventually led to a tragedy.

Cleopattera is airborne to catch up with JimBob

It was a Saturday morning, and our housecleaning lady had entered through the garage where the dogs had their own "bedroom" as the carpenter called it, that led to a 160' fenced run.

Suspecting she may have been careless, I immediately ran to the garage. JimBob and Cleopattera were missing. (Petite Chou was never more than a few feet away from me. Sometimes, when I would take a step, I would almost trip on her. We were inseparable.) After driving the neighborhood for two hours, I went home. Shortly afterward, the phone rang. A vet's office was calling to tell me that Cleopattera had been hit and killed by a car. The woman who hit her brought her to the vet but there was nothing they could do. The woman was distraught and said the little dog ran right in front of her car with the bigger dog following. Swallowing, I asked, "Did the big dog get hit, too?"

"No, she was able to miss him, but brought him along and we have him here. We'll hold him until you can pick him up." This was the first time I had a dog killed by a car. It's painful. You wake up in the morning and let them out, feed them, play with them. Each has its own personality and qualities. Each are equally precious. And then suddenly one is not there. There's a void. Gone forever, except for the memories, in Cleopattera's case, brief memories, but indelible for those of us who loved her. We know she is in Doggy Heaven, probably running ahead a pack of angel dogs. And we are thankful that JimBob couldn't keep up with her. It saved his life.

Now JimBob is about seven years old. He has health issues. He has emphysema, probably caused when he was lost in the fire. He has digestive problems and is on a special diet. He has intestinal problems. We see the vet frequently. One severe attack kept him in the hospital for a week. Friday afternoon, we brought him home, took margaritas out by the pool to relax and just enjoy the week-end with "Lovedog", his nickname. He and I began to stroll through the garden. Suddenly I saw what looked like a dead fish laying there. Yes, it was a big goldfish. Instinctively, I reached for it to prevent JimBob from grabbing it. After what he went through all week, and what it cost us, his devouring a decaying old dead fish was certainly to be avoided. But he was too quick for me. He swallowed it instantly.

It was Friday night. The vet was closed but I tried calling anyway and got put through as an emergency. We were told to bring him in immediately. The fish undoubtedly had bones that would cause grave damage. They pumped out his stomach and we returned home to what was left of the evening. He survived! The next day, I relayed the incident to our neighbor who said the fish was stolen from his pond of koi by possums and left the remnants on the patio. I told him it was ironic that for what we paid to have JimBob's stomach pumped out, we could have gone out for a nice fish dinner.

He responded by saying what that one koi cost him, we could have bought three or four fish dinners. Jack helped him cover the pond with chicken wire to keep the possums out—we didn't want any more dead fish incidents. These were wonderful neighbors who were extremely sensitive about their garden. After his wife saw a dead rat floating in her pool, she never went in it again.

Perhaps we underestimate the memories of dogs. JimBob had been with us for six years and was totally secure as part of our family. Yet, one day at the beach, he stared intensely at a van that pulled up. Someone got out and JimBob immediately took off at a fast run. He thought he recognized that person, probably his original owner. Tail wagging, he joyously rushed to that individual. After some serious sniffing, and a cool reception, he retreated back to us. But it is interesting that some residue of a relationship remains with an animal. It should be remembered by those who discard their pets so easily, that years later those pets could still be looking for them in a crowd. Still loving, unconditionally. Now JimBob's luck is running out. His liver isn't working. He's in and out of the vet's. Finally, the vet sent him home saying there wasn't anything else he could do for him. I asked if there was anything I could do for him. He said if I could get him to eat, he might make it.

I tried all his favorites...tiny bites of steak, ground up lamb, cantaloupe which he loved. Staying beside him on a blanket, I tried all night and through the next morning. He wouldn't or couldn't eat. I didn't know that he was in pain, I didn't know if or how much he was suffering. But not knowing was the reason I took him back for his final shot.

Cowardly, I waited outside and afterward went in for the final goodbye. JimBob would be the last dog I abandoned at the final moment. Even though it is unbelievably heart-wrenching, a dog wants to be with you to the last breath and that is the least I can do for someone who has so enriched my life, provided so much fun and laughter, so much devotion and love.

CHAPTER THREE

AN UNPARALLED INVESTMENT
Starring: PETITE CHOU

Now to tell her story. Petite Clou missed JimBob. If he stole her heart, she stole everyone else's. She was the most beautiful toy Poodle. I bought her a short time after I left Chicago, my home and family, and came to California. She was the only dog I ever bought—all the rest were shelter rescues or foundlings—aka dog-nappees. She was five weeks old. I was twenty-one. I clung to her as she was my only friend, my only family in this scary place called Hollywood. I went there to try for an acting career, but most of the time I was so intimidated, I stayed in the apartment with the shades drawn only to sneak her onto the bus for an outing in the local park.

She actually made friends for me and got me acclimated. I took her everywhere—shopping, to the gym, on dates to restaurants hidden in my lap. She was the star with her long perfect white ears that she would flip ala blonde Veronica Lake. The first time I had her formally trimmed, some friends wouldn't talk to me. They said I ruined her little-lamb look. Her name, translated literally, means "little cabbage" is a term of endearment that I heard on my first trip to Paris. That's what I was called.

Petite Chou's Little Lamb Look

Her favorite toy was actually a cat toy – a little fur muff with a tie and a bell. She would shake that muff, then let it fly off and run to retrieve it, repeating this routine over and over. Thoroughly entertaining was her running at full speed around and around the dining table, then throughout the house, room to room, like a white bullet. And if she wasn't moving, people thought she was a stuffed toy. But she was far too alive to be mistaken as a toy for long.

Guess which one is the toy
And which is Petite Chou!

The first time she got sick, with pneumonia, I cried and cried and cried. If I had to leave her for an interview and got stuck in traffic, I would 21 cry till I got home, worried that she was left alone too long.

I watched other dogs for potential attacks and would snatch her up on the slightest provocation.

Once, looking down at her, thinking that perhaps I should pick her up, I noticed she was arching her back as she did when I picked her up. Thereafter, I observed her getting the message that I was going to pick her up when I just *thought* about it and before I made the move. She would then prepare herself by arching her back, providing me with a little handle. Dogs are attuned to us so much more than we think. They see and watch everything in their territory. I've tried setting a toy on a shelf without saying anything. Not just one but many of my dogs did the same thing—just sat there, staring. Knowing it was for them and just waiting for the gift.

Chouchie, which was her nickname, also watched for signs that I might leave. Putting on make-up, she would sit on my feet. Bringing the luggage out had her hiding under the bed, although she always went with me. To France, to New York, Chicago, even Las Vegas. If you ever want to *really* have a good time in France, take your dog. A special promotion with Air France allowed me to take her on First Class. In Parisian restaurants, she got her own seat and plate on which she was served delicious tidbits, sent from the kitchen. At the hotels, bellboys would vie for the *honor* of walking her, showing off the little toy that strutted and then, nose down, would sniff the special aromas of France.

Petite Chou goes first class to Paris.

I took her to the House of Balenciaga where I was being fitted for a gown. Cristabal Balenciaga was one of the three greatest designers in the world of fashion. It's difficult to describe how rarified the atmosphere is in those ateliers. Clients are treated reverentially, as if royalty. And frequently were royalty. Stepping out of a garment, someone is there to balance you, holding your elbow, someone to pick it up, hang it. Someone to assist you in trying on the new creation. It was such an exotic experience, I forgot about Chouchie. She had snuck out of the fitting room and turned up where – naturally, in Balenciaga's room where he worked in solitude with no interruptions allowed. The relieved and surprised vendeuse returned from the search with her, saying "Monsieur was *charmed* by her." As we all were.

One other time she escaped from me in a department store. I looked around to find her doing her business behind a counter standing right next to a saleslady who had not yet seen her. I quickly rushed over, and with the only thing I had, a used tissue in my pocket, I picked it up and retreated to my friend, asking if he had ever held a hot turd in his hand. I should add here that in her 17 years, there were only a few such indiscretions. She was a lady and acted like it at all times.

Flying to New York, I hid her in a big purse. After we took off, she came out and crawled up on my shoulder to look around. Now exposed, everyone in the cabin wanted to hold her, and she was passed from seat to seat, and giving each person a genuine dose of that charm, while the flight attendant gave me disapproving looks. New York was fun for her—all those intriguing city scents. You don't have to feel sorry for those dogs in New York.

Cloistered in better off than those dogs locked in backyards, with little human contact except at feeding time. And people in New York should get along as well as all the dogs do. You see the professional walkers out with a long string of varied breeds and sizes, happy as can be and not the slightest bit aggressive.

Flying to Las Vegas with my father-in-law, I wrapped her in a yellow satin baby blanket. The flight attendant oohhhh'ed and asked if she could see the baby. I said she was sleeping and continued on board while my traveling companion blushed with embarrassment. O.K, so I was shameless! I know there are others who will commit crimes to keep their dog with them.

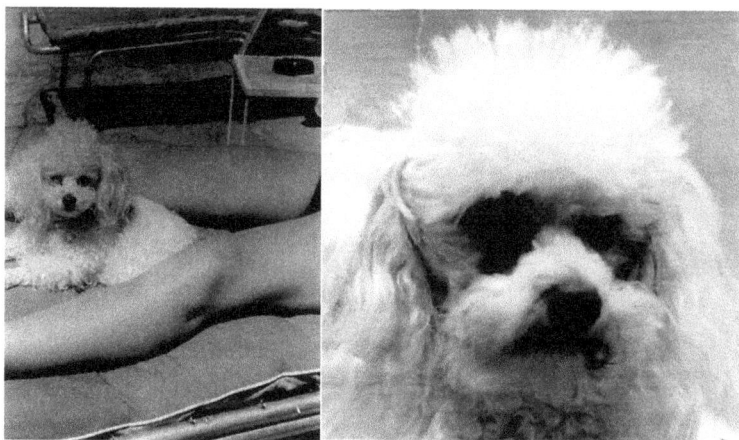

She liked to sunbathe with Lori and got the cutest freckles on her pink skin.

We boarded Air France for our return trip only to hear that we were being evicted because only one dog was allowed in First Class. One dog was already on and that dog had priority. What a relief to see the other dog person was none other than our friend, Mrs. Boeri, the wife of the head of Air France, USA. Seeing it was us, she told them it would be okay to have the second dog on board, saving us deplaning, delays and boundless complications. Mrs. Boeri, although married to a Frenchman, was English. When she returned home for a visit, of course taking her little poodle, she flew to Scotland, rented a car and drove to England, which was illegal because dogs entering England had to be impounded for six months. But who would ever subject their beloved dog to that?

It's known that poodles are the smartest of breeds. I love the story about the intelligence test they gave some breeds to determine which was smarter. The test was a series of barricades and the dogs had to figure out a way to get over it. The German Shepherd, the Rottweiler, and Doberman all struggled through the maze. The poodle surveyed the scene for a while and then just walked *around it*, test your dog on the next walk when it gets tangled up with a tree, fire hydrant or lamp post. Does it pull and tug, or just wait for you to untangle it? Or, like Petite Chou, does it reverse course, and untangle itself?

Dogs are probably like Yogi Berra, who said, "You could observe a lot just by watching." Well, dogs watch EVERYTHING. They read you like a book. But more than that, I believe they are very intuitive if you allow them to bond with you. By bond, I mean a special emotional tie. Like when you are depressed or lonely, your dog will come and lay by you so you feel its warmth and lick your hand. And the intuitive bond goes both ways, like when you get the feeling that something isn't quite right. Checking your pet, you discover a suspicious lump or an ear that is infected. Yes, the intuitioncommunication goes both ways. We just need to be receptive.

| A little girl hugs Petite Chou. | Petite Chou gives Lori a kiss. | She's Lori's constant companion. |

There were only a few people I would leave Petite Chou with if I had to go out of town. My in-laws adored her and took their meals with her standing on the table, sharing their food, spoiling her shamelessly. They took her shopping to the pet stores, buying a wardrobe of colorful and jeweled collars and leashes.

I also trusted my closest friend, Raven. With waist-long shining black hair, warm dark eyes, a sensitivity along with an exotic aura, she exuded spirituality, humor, and intelligence. She and Petite Chou were soulmates. But Raven was a night person and couldn't get moved into our house early on the morning we left for Hawaii. So Petite Chou stood alone at the window as she watched us leave. As we drove away, my friend asked me, "Are you crying?" Of course, I was. It broke my heart to leave her. As soon as we landed, I rushed to telephone home and Raven assured me they were just fine so I could continue on and enjoy my vacation.

A week later, returning early morning, they were both still in bed. Petite Chou rushed to the edge and wiggled—no—vibrated her delight to have me back. Suddenly she stopped and looked off with a vacant stare. She often did that when trying to remember where her toy was. (In fact, most of my dogs will stop, as if to think, suddenly remember and then retrieve something.) Then she turned and ran back to Raven. We exchanged knowing looks. She didn't want Raven to think she had forgotten her. She told us that she cared about both of us. But she was always concerned about me.

Meeting a handsome young man in a Hollywood club, he took me home and invited himself in. One moment we were sitting on the sofa and the next I was flat on my back, struggling, about to be raped. I started to cry. Petite Chou jumped up on the sofa and began to lick my face. It must have moved him, because he stopped and disappeared into the bathroom for a long time. I could hear him going through my medicine cabinet. Then he left. Petite Chou had saved me.

Petite Chou goes for a ride in her own

Petite Chou is cuddled by actor Richard

CHAPTER FOUR

Petite Chou Meets a Movie Star
(Well, a TV Star)

I hadn't thought about breeding her until a woman approached me in a department store, telling me they had a super well-bred, male Toy Poodle and asked if I would be interested in breeding my dog. Then she told me she was the wife of a big tv star, Rick Jason, and invited us to their home in Beverly Hills. *I'd get to meet my first movie star in California, see inside my first Beverly Hills mansion and maybe there would be a little Petite Chou!* I was so impressed with everything and enamored with the dark, handsome Rick Jason that I hardly noticed and certainly didn't comment on the fact that "Tinker" was almost twice Petite's size, and he was definitely not in her "perfect" class. The two got along just fine and I agreed that if they did breed, they would get pick of the litter. And that was the beginning of the total domination of both Petite Chou and me.

The first thing I was told to do is have her tear glands removed because they caused dark stains on her face. Not knowing the vet or anything about the procedure, I obeyed. And paid a hefty fee, not exactly easy for a struggling actress. They stayed in close contact, hoping to hear that the moment had come. There was a long lecture on the need for timing from Rick who had become the expert in all things pertinent to breeding. So at just the right moment, I took her to their home and left her while Rick supervised the event. Returning several hours later, there was a full report: Tinker couldn't do it and Rick had to help. Then Tinker did get it and there was a two hour "locked" union. It seemed like Petite Chou was more than glad to get out of there.

We were required to make trips to the vet for pre-natal care. I ate a lot of macaroni and cheese to economize, and made daily reports on every little detail which the Jason's relished. At 1 A.M. on a Friday, I heard her scratching under the bed. She was trying to make a nest so she was getting ready to deliver. As promised, I called them to report the news. They were at my doorstep in what seemed like minutes. By this time, the first tiny puppy had rolled out quite easily. Petite Chou did all the things a good mother does and then started to behave strangely, we thought. She would get up, circle and lie down again, over and over. Rick immediately had his vet on the phone, who explained that she was in labor and there was going to be another puppy. The minutes rolled by and the second puppy did not emerge. Over and over, she would get up, circle and lay down again, trying to encourage the birth—all with a rapt audience. An hour later, it began to emerge but ever so slowly. It was coming out with great difficulty and it was big! This was an unintended consequence of my blundering. Finally, it plopped out and it looked just like Tinker. Mission accomplished.

I was given instructions on the post-natal care. Rick insisted I give her a teaspoon of honey which would re-energize her to care for the pups. My advice to all would-be breeders is "Don't do it!" She had just gone through a long ordeal, was busy caring for her babies, and now her face was sticky, even the nest was smeared with honey. But the ensuing mess was not their problem. They left and it took days to clean her up.

Although most breeders sell their pups at six weeks, they insisted I keep them for three months to make sure they were nurtured. By that time, Petite Chou was tired of them and when they tried to nurse, she jumped out of the box. They sold their "pick of the litter", the first and beautiful little guy, to a friend in New York. I sold my "Tinker, Jr." to a lady with a tie store on Melrose, referred to by the Jasons for a fraction of what they got, but it was over and I would never again be tempted to breed her. She had to be relieved.

Debie and Lori in pool

CHAPTER FIVE

Reminiscing

The years went by. Seventeen of them. We went to Chicago to visit my retired parents. I knew my Dad would love her. He loved dogs period which probably is where I get it from. But his dog, Patches, did not and got even with me for bringing in competition by throwing up in my slippers. My Dad had been a machinist but he also had done house painting as a side job. Our neighbors asked him to paint their house and when they wanted to pay him, he told them in lieu of money, he would like to take the dog they had tied up in the garage. He thought that was abusive and preferred to save her rather take than the money.

"Trixie", a big beautiful German shepherd would be the pride and joy of the family for many years. I grew up with her. We played house, with her sitting by a little table and being served in tiny toy dishes. We played in the snow and she would bound through high drifts to retrieve a stick. If there were no stick, she would yank a twig out of the ground. She helped my little sister learn to walk by letting her hang on, and then patiently took a step at a time.

Trixie, the German Shepherd, and
12-year Lori play in the snow.

Today we know better than to give our dogs bones of any kind, but back then we fed our dog table scraps. Once a bone got stuck in her throat. The family sat, frozen, not knowing what to do as she choked. I grabbed her, put my hand down her throat until I felt the bone and gently removed it. Everyone was shocked that a little kid would know what to do. But she was my dog! When I grew up and had a place of my own, I became convinced that I would give her a better home than my parents, so I took her with me. She was not at all convinced and spent the entire time at the door, waiting to go to the home and family she loved. My mother complained all the time about the fur that was shed year round. She was continually sweeping it up.

Although my Dad totally loved Mom, in a contest, she risked losing, because his dogs—and there were many of them—were important to him. He cared so much about them.

There was Chickie who we took her in because she was old and nobody wanted her. She may have been abused because she was a "snapper" and we had to be careful. But not so old because the following year she somehow presented us with a litter of puppies.

I was probably about seven when we had Silver (ala HiHo Silver and Tonto – remember?) Anyway I can't forget Silver because he got his leg caught in some barbed wire and was screaming in pain. When I tried to free his leg, he snapped at me. I pulled my hand away but caught it on the barbed wire and still have a substantial scar to remind me of him.

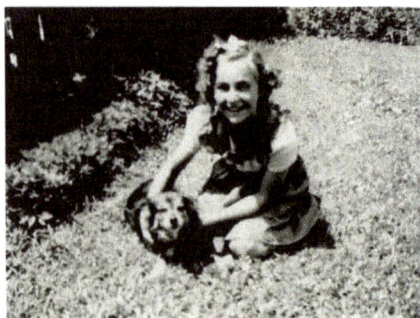

The "aged" Chickie and 8 year old Lori

Chickie's puppy and 10 year Lori pose for the camera

I remember Mickey, Mousey, and Snoopy, so named long before Charles Schultz but there were many more whose names I've forgotten. But if my Dad and I loved dogs, my brother, Bill, loved cats. He had an aloof yellow cat named Tiger whose tail was permanently bent at a 45 degree angle. We had found her with a long string of cans tied to her tail just in time to save that tail from breaking off. That was a cruel game played by juvenile delinquents. Bill went into the army in 1942 and we kept Tiger going during the four years he spent mostly in the jungles of the South Pacific. She was there to greet him on his return. When he moved to Fox Lake, he started collecting cats with a vengeance. He kept an old car where dozens lived. The tree next to his house would fill up with cats, sitting on the branches, looking just like a flock of magpies. These were not house pets. They were wild and yet he insisted on naming each one, picking them up, petting them and then being punished with fearful scratches—daily. He always had stories to tell about his cats—how and where he found them. The one I liked the most was when he bought a nice fish for his dinner and odds and ends from the butcher for the cats. Tasting his fine fish, he decided he didn't like it and ran out to see if he could salvage some of the cat's fish. No luck. They ate it all. He was quite put out about it.

Brother Bill pets the kitties A few of Bill's cats being whether they like it or not being fed in the garden.

Mostly, *Not!* Grandma and Mom watch in amazement.

Trixie was about twelve when her swollen leg was diagnosed as bone cancer. In fact, most of the leg bone had been consumed by the disease. She was so alive that putting her down seemed impossible so we opted for surgery—removing the leg, leaving her with three. She came home from surgery and resumed her usual activities of retrieving sticks without a complaint.

Lori's Mom and Dad with two of the many dogs they made homes for.

Two more—Buddy and Mickey

After some years, Trixie's body began to fail. This was going to be bad, but Dad made the decision to end her suffering. Although still a teenager, he asked me to drive them to the vet. Trixie, in the back seat, was very aware something was happening. With Dad's lower lip trembling, we took her in. He told them we would wait outside. We smoked a cigarette while he said he would go back in to make sure she had been put to sleep to make sure that she would not be used for experiments. That was amazing perception. There was no common awareness of dogs being sold to labs for experimentation back in the early fifties. How did he know about the threat? But he would make sure for Trixie so we went back in and confirmed her demise. Ironically, my brother told me that shortly after my Dad died, my mother had Animal Control pick up his dog, Patches, who by this time, was old and feeble. But whatever happened to her, I know they're together now in Doggie Heaven—my Dad, Patches, Trixie and all the others too numerous to name here. And lest we judge my mother too harshly, we must acknowledge that she spent her entire life with my father sweeping up the shedding fur.

If humans have been blessed with dogs, the curse has been the difference in lifespans. Part of the relationship is preparing for the separation that will predictably take place. Dolphins can live to the eighties, elephants, ravens, turtles have many times the lifespan our beloved pets who can barely make it to ten years even if we try to protect them from disease and accidents. And tragedy does strike!

For seventeen years, Petite Chou was coddled and pampered. A distended tummy mean an emergency trip to the vets, always anticipating the worst which would usually turn out to be an attack of gas. Coughing on Catalina had us on the midnight ferry and rushing to an all-night vet. Every precaution was taken to protect her from aggressive dogs, even cats, unhealthy food. And yet—-yet, she drowned in our pool. Mostly blind and deaf, she hardly ever left her heating pad. Not finding her anywhere in the house, I panicked and looked in the garden. She wasn't there. Then I passed the pool. There she was, her beautiful white body floating in the moonlight.

People were kind to me. Her vet suggested she died instantly of a heart attack when hitting the icy cold water. A friend suggested she committed suicide. I wrapped her in the yellow satin baby blanket and Jack dug a grave under a tree in the garden. The first time it rained, I could only stare out the window at that grave, thinking…

The next summer when I went into the pool for the first time, it was torture as I tried to imagine what her last moments were like. But

I think I know what they were because something very unusual happened to me that day—what can only be described as a psychic experience.

I'd had other psychic experiences, most of them as a child even though I probably didn't know it at the time, like the dream about a bird in trouble in a tree. The next morning, I looked in the tree next to our house and there was a bird, dangling upside down from a string that somehow had gotten tangled around its leg. I ran for a neighbor who climbed the tree, freed the bird, took it home, wrapped it in a towel to keep it warm and fed it liquids until it was strong enough to fly away. Then I continued on my way to sixth grade classes.

But the experience I had the day Petite Chou died was stranger than anything I had ever experienced and caused me to wonder at the time. I left to go to my office in Hollywood and while driving, I felt a sensation that was neither threatening nor invasive. Rather it was kind of warm and soft, starting in my toes and moving slowly up through my entire body with a gentle touch. The next day, reflecting on it, I realized there could only be one simple and logical explanation. I had no doubt that it was Petite Chou saying good-bye to me.

Twenty years later, I still dream about her, always the same dream. She has been lost. I find her in the back of a closet or hidden under something. She is unbelievably old by this time and frail. I set about to nourish and rejuvenate her. When I wake up, it isn't sad because I had her back. Even if it was only for a short time and in my dreams, I had her back with me.

Bobo at the beach

Bobo and Lori Take a ride

CHAPTER SIX

Dognapping In Our Front Yard:
Starring Cindy Lou, AKA Woozie the Woozle.

After that, you don't just go out and get another dog. I didn't know when, and if I ever would have again, if Jack had not found "that cute little dog hiding under the car." Enjoying a Sunday morning relaxing in bed, Jack came in saying the little dog hiding under his car was soooo cute. I said, "Bring her into the backyard." Moments later, a frenzied Australian sheepdog was leaping straight up in the air to peer at me through the windows. Up and down she went like a yo-yo. And she wasn't small! She was about a year old, no tags and hyper. One had to be cautious with her because at the slightest provocation, her kidneys could unleash. Jack named her Cindy Lou. One day, out of sheer frustration with her hyper-ness, I said, "She's a-A-A-WOOZIE. The name stuck. She was to become known as the notorious Woozie the Woozle! The center of Jack's universe and thief of my heart!

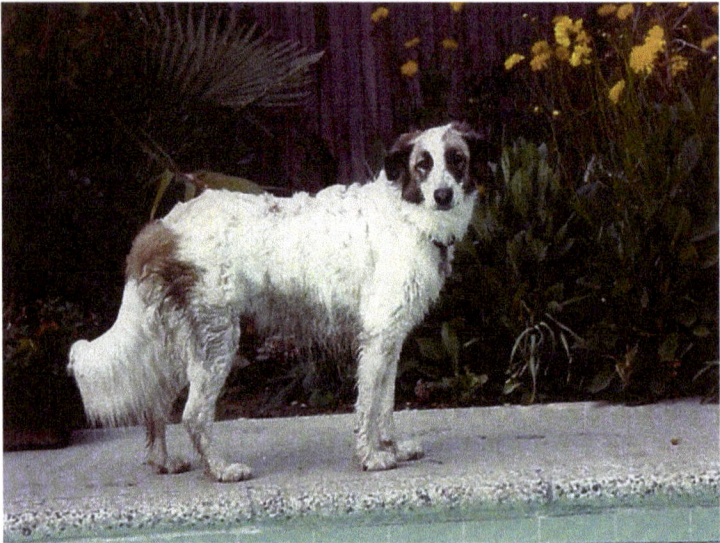

CINDY LOU, aka Woozie, the Woozle

She brought life and laughter back to our home. A fly was an enemy she could dedicate herself to catching. Bees she swallowed whole as if they were snacks. And she loved to get in the garbage so much we nicknamed her "Garbaggio". I am pretty sure that one time she swallowed a razor blade. There were no consequences so we assumed the other garbage she ate dissolved the blade somewhat like a goat's ability to digest just about anything.

"Sammy" squirrel provided her with delightful chases. We named him because by this time we knew him. And he knew her. In fact, of all our dogs who participated in the chase that went on for years, she was the only one who ever caught him. He made the mistake of getting off the telephone wires. As she proudly pranced with her prize, our other dogs watched jealously.

When we first got her, our good friend, Nat Davis, came immediately to see her. He walked in the door and she started barking. Relentlessly. Quickly, Nat sat down. His slightest movement would trigger another round of barking. She didn't know him, but there was something about him she didn't like. He is tall, 6.4, and that may have been a factor, but Nat is a consummate lover of dogs. In fact, he likes to say he got married so he could finally fulfill a lifelong dream of getting a "Collie dog". He married Lynn and they got Bruce, the most beautiful, elegant gentlemen Collie ever. So someone who looked like Nat must have abused Woozie and if dogs remember unconditionally loving someone, they also remember cruelty. If only they could talk. But they can't so we have the mystery of why dogs will react negatively sometimes. And why Woozie hurt Nat's feelings.

Woozie loved going to the beach. Seeing me out in the waves, she'd rush in, swim over to me, then turn around and go back, as if she had at least tried to herd me which was her most powerful instinct. Except for that one incident when she barked at Nat if he moved, there was never a problem with any aggressiveness—until a ten year old boy attempted to run past us while we were on our walk. Woozie had been concentrating on sniffs, so she was surprised and reacted by charging him. Sheepdogs don't bite, they herd and she wanted to teach him a lesson. He was terrified, of course, and retreated.

Later, our doorbell rang. It was the little boy and his mother. She was in a rage, telling me that my dog had bitten her little boy. I looked at him. He looked away. He lied! Woozie didn't bite him! So I said, "It wasn't my dog. We haven't been out of the house." She apologized and left.

Woozie, swimming through the surf to get her ball.

Wozzie checks out a flea laden puppy.

And signals approval.

Woozie stays at a mountain lodge with skier Lori.

CHAPTER SEVEN

Dog-napping by Request: Starring *Freddie*
(Who Just Wanted to be with Woozie)

It was a Sunday morning and Woozie and I went on an extended walk to an affluent neighborhood of large estates. I noticed a little dog behind us. Blocks later, he was still following. Finally, he caught up with us, ignoring me but vastly interested in Woozie, who was about three times his size. He was so cute and clean, I figured that he lived on one of the estates so I chased him, trying to discourage him from following as we headed home. He was not to be deterred. He followed, but sneakily on the other side of the street. We ran, we hid, but he stayed hot on our trail. When we finally crossed the street to our house, he followed. He had no tag. I figured *I've got another dog.*

Freddie—it's easy to see his Determination.

But Jack had other ideas and placed a Lost Dog ad in the local newspaper. A woman who lived in the estate area responded. She had found him earlier, in terrible shape and cleaned him up. She, too, had placed an ad and the real owners responded. The story was that he belonged to a big family living in Glendale which is 25 miles on the other side of the valley. They had just lost another bigger dog who was the little one's best friend. Supposedly, he escaped from the car window they left open to look for his lost best friend. The woman who called me gave me the owners' number. Then she wondered if he should go back because he was the second dog they lost, probably through carelessness. And if I didn't want to return him to the owners, she would be glad to have him back. In other words, she wanted him!

Well, so did I! But by this time, Freddie, that's what I called him, after the late Fred Allen because he was such a comedian, was settled in and totally happy with Woozie. She was the replacement for his lost friend. I rationalized like crazy, finally deciding that he would have a better home with us. The fact is I never met a dog I didn't want to take home with me. So I had little Freddie and he had Woozie. We were a happy little family and now I deserved my nickname: "Dog-napper".

My, what big teeth you have, Woozie!

My, what big teeth *you* have, Freddie.

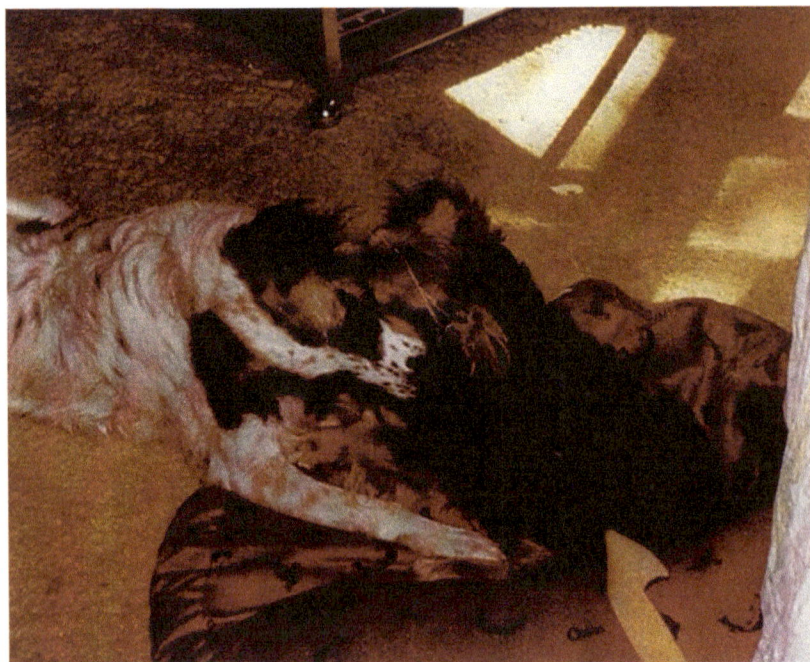

Hey, we're just having fun!

Sometimes I did give them back. Once I took home a very tall Irish Setter who was galloping across Ventura Boulevard and around the carwash. No one there knew who she belonged to, but she was injured. one there knew who she belonged to but she was injured. She didn't get into my car, she leaped into it and from then on, everything was a leap. At home, she immediately leaped into our pool, swan a length, got out, shook and leaped up on the sofa. She loved water. Once I found her actually putting a toy in the toilet, thereafter keeping the lid down. After our vet stitched her up, he discovered stitches still in her from a hysterectomy which he removed. The bill was substantial.

She, too, got settled in our home which seemed to be Dog Heaven, but we still did the ad thing. A young man called and after a thorough description, I had to admit it was his dog. Or rather his wife's dog. After they married, the dog was exiled to permanent residence in the backyard. She had shared her mistress's bed prior to the wedding. Of course, she was upset and wanted to escape. The young man assured me that she would be included in their home from then on. So I gave him directions to our house, hung up and waited. And waited and waited. Did he change his mind? Did he get lost? I thought I heard someone yelling on the street and opened the door to see a man calling his dog. It was him, of course, because although I gave him directions to the house, I didn't give the address. So all he could do is go up and down the street calling his dog. Was there some unconscious motivation there?

After relaying the story to him of his I found her, I let him have his dog back. Now he wanted to reward me. I said that wasn't necessary, we had enjoyed her and were glad to have been able to save her from a terrible fate. He insisted and kept insisting that he wanted to reward me for all my efforts and taking out his wallet, pulled out a five dollar bill and handed it to me. Of course, I declined and at least this time I didn't "dog-nap". I should also get credit for other times I didn't dog-nap. For instance, I was driving in Hollywood and noticed a big German Shepherd about to either fall or jump out of a pick-up truck. I pulled up next to the truck, rolled down my window and called over a warning. The driver snarled back at me, "Mind your own business, lady" and he stomped on the gas pedal to take off. I continued but happened to glance in the rear-view mirror and there was the German Shepherd, standing in the middle of the road, looking confused. Now I had a dilemma. If I went back for him, I would be late for my session in the recording studio at umpteen dollars a minute. Oh, well!

Warily, he jumped in the back seat and eyed me suspiciously. He was huge and definitely not the kind of dog you would reach over and pet. Then he had a reaction, indicating that he liked me. He liked me ALOT! Now to catch the truck! Racing down the street and turning left, I saw the truck turning. Again, I raced only to see him turning again. Catching him seemed impossible. Finally overtaking him by driving at unlawful speed, I 59 pointed to the backseat. He did a double take and pulled over to stop. Jumping out, he ran to his dog. He was crying with joy and humbly thanked me. Best of all, he promised that "Lucky" would forever ride in the front seat with him.

We learned to take a box of dog cookies when traveling, because if there is a lost dog somewhere, I will find it. Or it will find me. There were lots of stray dogs in Hawaii—they're called poi dogs. Taking a dog to Hawaii meant it had to endure six months of quarantine. This resulted in very few new dogs and lots of in-breeding and in general a casual attitude about caring for them. The dogs were very sweet. There was one I fell in love with and wanted to take home. When I got home, I called the hotel to see if they could find the dog for me. The dog was gone. I called the vet in Maui for advice and he assured me that Hawaiians were very kind and that "my dog" would come to no harm but would probably live a good life in the gentle climate. Since he swam with me every day and loved the water, I knew he would at least stay free of fleas and ticks and resulting diseases. That gave me some comfort.

Two "poi" dogs at the beach on Maui

The black "poi" dog comes for a visit

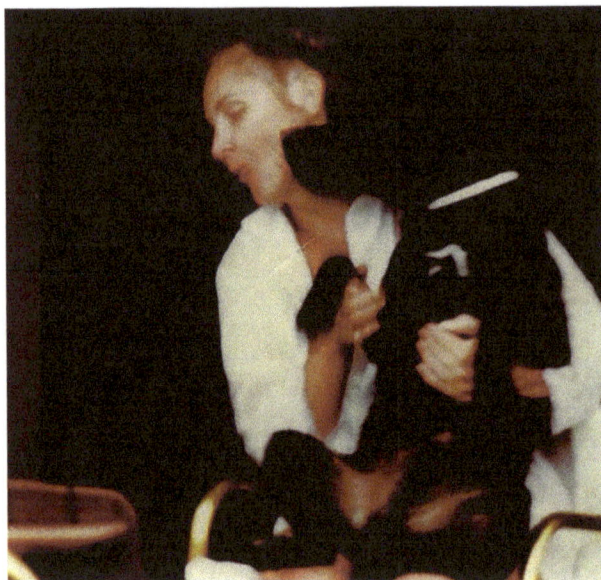

Two "poi" dog become good friends

Traveling to different parts of the world can be difficult for those of us who are dog-sensitive. Dogs are still considered meat in some countries. I don't know if I would ever recover from seeing little dogs being sold in the markets in China or Korea where dogmeat is thought to increase a man's prowess. And although the prospect of an increasing population of Muslims may bode as bad news to dogs who are considered "unclean", we can hope that modern Muslims refer back to Mohammed, who said the woman at the well who shared the water with a thirsty dog had earned a place in heaven.

Clearly, the more affluent countries have a culture of loving dogs with the one exception of parts of Switzerland, where dog meat is still used for sausages. The worst international experience I had was in Baja, Mexico, where bands of dogs run wild. And incredibly diseased.

We saw a group and someone quickly said to me, "Don't look". But I already had and suddenly felt sick. It is almost impossible to imagine dogs so diseased, so bloody, so full of gushing sores and obviously and living off garbage or starving. Mexico gets help from Doctors without Borders. Doctors, using small planes, volunteer their services and fly there to help in the most remote areas. They could use a Vet without Borders, too. However, our vets do have a practice of sending any medicine that is past its expiration date to vets down there. Any that we have left over in our house, we give to our vet to send, too. Every bit helps.

And while we're focused on dogs, I would like to add something about horses and the people who own them for the purpose of riding

– their entertainment. I only hope that you are prepared to care for your horse when you can no longer ride it because it has arthritis, or other physical problems not to mention just plain getting tired of it. Sugar brought this to my attention a few years ago. She was a lovely white horse, kept it on a corner lot that I passed when I did my daily walk. She was there 24-7. She had no barn, no shelter of any kind. That was the year we had El Nino and it rained for months. She would be out there with the rain just pouring down on her. I brought her carrots every day. Eventually, she'd watch for me.

Sugar checks Lori's pocket for a carrot.

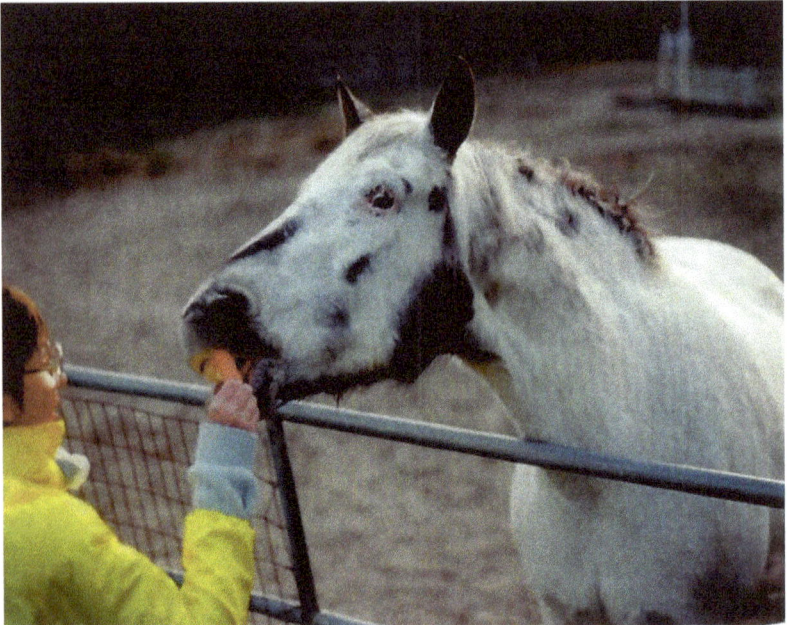

Sugar gets her carrot!

I've had some interesting experiences with horses, too, which is why I relate to them. At a New York City parade, I noticed that a policeman was astride a most wonderful horse. She had something. I looked at her and she looked back. We made contact and I said, "Hello". She began to move toward me. My friend looked at me. The officer looked at me. To his chagrin, he could not stop his horse from coming to see me. Considering how well those traffic horses are trained, she had to have been mightily motivated. But once she got to me and we had a nice petting-chit-chat session, she was satisfied and followed instructions to move back in line. The way I saw it, she wasn't any different from anybody else. Somebody says a friendly "hello", you stop for a visit. Especially if you like someone and I do think she liked me. Because she knew I liked her. Contact!

When I couldn't stand Sugar's situation any more, I inquired at the house on the property. They didn't own the horse, merely leased the space to the horse's owner. The owner was a young girl who had moved "up" to a younger, better horse. And besides that, Sugar had arthritis. Treating it cost $200 a month plus $200 a month for food made her a bad investment with little entertainment return.

I considered trying to buy Sugar but $400 a month plus placing her in a decent stable was beyond my means. Shortly after my conversations with the owner, she was sold, probably to another young person who will use her and then move on, and eventually, we know where Sugar will go. So I have one thing to say to riders who don't commit themselves to caring and feeding for the living animal that gives them so much pleasure. If you just want a ride, get something that you can buy replacement parts for when it has a problem. Get something that doesn't have any feelings, that won't develop affection and loyalty for you and grieve when you trade it in on a newer, better model. Get something that's okay to condemn to a constant churning of owners-homes and ultimately the scrapheap. In other words, just get A CAR. Or a bike. Or a motorcycle.

CHAPTER EIGHT

Dog-napping Amongst the Mansions:
Starring Three Puppies

The following week-end Woozie and I did the same walk to the big estate area, leaving Freddie at home, lest he might escape again. Walking by almost the same spot where I first saw Freddie, a big dog began to follow us. Then, hearing a growl in the nearby bushes, I looked to see the source of the growl. A snarling head popped up. It looked like a Doberman. The big dog following us took off. We continued our walk. On the way back, we stopped at the bushes and up popped the head again, this time not growling but friendly. Woozie and I pushed into the bushes to investigate and there it was, a Doberman puppy. And with him was another puppy, a female black lab. Some rustling and a male black lab emerged. These puppies were so adorable. Oh, dear, what to do. It was hard but after a lot of petting, we finally left them and ran home to tell Jack the news. "Well, dear, in the past two weeks, we've gotten one new dog so now we have two. How about three more?"

The response was negative. Someone else would find them and to forget it. Well, I tried but by 5 P.M., I was thinking that while the Doberman puppy was brave in scaring off the big dog, he was no match for the coyotes who would soon be patrolling the streets. The three of them would make a feast for the pack. Jack never could stand my weeping, so he agreed to go back with me. They were still there and you never saw such wiggles. Jack also noticed a big bucket of dogfood probably left by whoever abandoned them, anticipating it would keep them going until one of the "rich estate" people took them in, a cruel but common practice. We took them home with the agreement that they had to stay outside.

Three adorable black puppies, probably about six

If you think one puppy is cute, you should try three sometime. It was enchantment. Each had its own personality. The Doberman, who was really a kind of Rottweiler-Labrador-German Shepherd-Doberman mix, was clearly dominant. Anyway, we called him Dobbie. The male lab was quite shy and was named Sonny. He would hide in back of me and chew on my hair while I played with the others. The female, named Sissy, was sweet. Slowly they worked their way into the house and we realized we now had five dogs.

Trying to do housework was no small challenge. Like trying to make a bed with dogs having a great time leaping on it and tunneling under the covers. Everything, including sweeping the floor, was a game. One day I was so frustrated, I did a "time-out" and put them in the car, expecting the confinement to calm them down. Boy, was I in for a surprise. Not to be deterred from mischief, they demolished the back seat – chewed it into pieces. When I opened the back, I saw bits of upholstery and stuffing flying out the window. It's times like these that you have to remember how rewarding having dogs can be. At the time I was producing commercials for Zero Pet Control, an organization financed by the city so supposedly I had good contacts for finding homes. One woman was highly recommended. They said she took in many dogs and gave them not just care but love and personal attention. She just asked for a donation of dogfood. Thinking she would be our salvation, I bought several huge bags of dogfood and drove to her home in L.A. and rang the doorbell. No dogs barked and none came to the door when a woman opened it. I asked her where the dogs were and was shown to the backyard. Our presence brought dozens of dogs crawling out from the foundation. Her husband was told to bring the dogs in and when we went to the car, he pulled on gloves, presumably so as not to dirty his hands. He grabbed Sissy's leg and pulled her out. One by one, he brusquely transferred them to the backyard. I was in shock. This was supposed to be a loving, caring refuge not a stockyard. I left them, and got on the freeway. "No!" I announced to myself and At the first offramp I announced to myself "No!" got off, turned around, went back and retrieved Dobbie, Sissy and Sonny. We had to do better for them . We were back to five dogs.

One night I woke up to hear intense growling coming from outside where they still had to sleep. I found Sonny, lying on the concrete, shivering, while Dobbie and Sissy stayed warm in the big doghouse with Dobbie growling to tell Sonny he couldn't come in.

I should have known to expect trouble. Two males and one female and Dobbie bigger and dominant! Giving Sonny an old bathrobe to sleep on, I went back to bed, thinking all was settled. Next morning, guess who was curled up on my bathrobe while Sonny and Sissy snuggled in the doghouse. Discovering the bathrobe, Dobbie must have considered it a special privilege and of course, commandeered it for himself. It was becoming apparent that Dobbie would be the first to go.

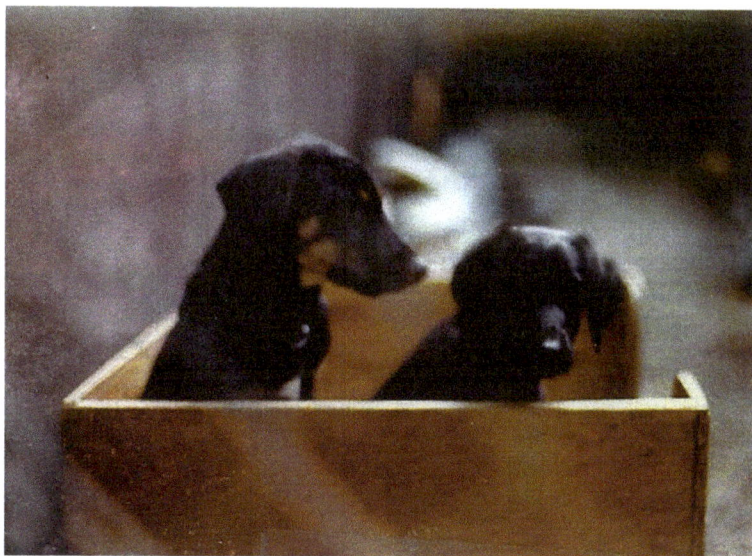

Dobbie and Sissy sharing a box. Sonny, left out and shivering in the cold

Not knowing that you literally can't give away big black dogs, especially Dobermans, I placed an ad written carefully to sound appealing. Not one response. No one wanted Dobbie. But there was a call for a female so I drove to inspect the family and house, Sissy

65

ensconced on my lap. They were lovely with two well-behaved children who took to Sissy immediately. She wasn't at all upset when I got up to leave. But I was and burst into tears. The two children stared at me, an adult, sobbing like a little baby. I called them occasionally over the next year. It was all good news. Sissy was part of their family.

Now we had four dogs, in terms of seniority, Woozie, Freddie, Dobbie and Sonny. One female, two males. It was clear to Sonny and Woozie that Dobbie·was the leader of the pack. With Freddie, it wasn't clear at all. He hated Dobbie. That little guy bullied the ninety pounder. He'd stare and growl aggressively. Dobbie, good leader that he was, avoided confrontation, and did his best to placate him. When Freddie harassed him, he'd turn away to face the wall, a sign of non-aggression. But when it came to his "pack", Dobbie was tough on other dogs actually biting a few. That changed one day when I was in the garden picking bouquet of calla lilies and Dobie decided he had enough and fought back. Freddie didn't back down and the only thing I could do was swat them with the calla lilies. It did break up the fight and I'm sure it made a hilarious scene but we know Dobbie could have ended it quickly with one bite of little Freddie. Thank heaven he exercised an "alpha dog's restraint and humored him.

Dobbie, the alpha male who really tried to get along with Freddie.

Dobie, proving he needed training.

Wozzie isn't in this picture, but she was watching from a window as Dobbie and the others were being trained. Amazingly, she learned everything they did, proving how smart Australian Sheepdogs are.

On a Friday night, I left the office early to go home, enjoy the weekend by the pool, with My dogs. I sat on the sofa with a margarita. Dobbie jumped up by me and cuddled. Freddie, competitive as always, jumped up and snarled. Quickly, Dobbie exited the sofa and ran for the garden. The problem was that sliding glass doors were between him and the garden. They were closed. He hit fast and hard. Stunned, he stopped for a moment. I watched, paralyzed, as the glass began to slide down—with Dobie right under it. He then proceeded through the door, saving his life by an instant. Once again on Friday night, we rushed to Emergency to have stitches put in his head.

I swear he was jinxed. His first puppy walks had him tripping up curbs with those huge feet. He collided with a rose bush and carried the resulting bump on his head to the end. One day we came home to find blood on the floor. An inspection revealed two holes in Dobbie. Sonny was blamed for fighting with Dobbie. By the time we got him to Emergency, he was in shock. We discovered that the holes weren't from a fight with Sonny. They were from the two bullets that some kindly neighbor put in him and they were too close to the spine to be removed. Like I said, people just don't like big, black dogs.

The next year our doorbell rang and a young woman said she had accidentally hit a dog and wondered if it was ours. No, I said, because ours were all present and accounted for. But I didn't know that Dobbie had been out earlier. Sometime later, I said I smelled blood. "Blood doesn't smell," I was told. Insisting, everyone was inspected and lo and behold, it was Dobbie who got hit and had his belly scraped by the car. By this time I noticed our vet had expanded the hospital. It even had a big electric sign—Emergency Care. I believe we have a vested interest in that sign. I drove a Toyota Celica with a hatchback and sunroof. All five of us would pile in and drive a mile for a run in a manicured, grassy landfill that went for acres and acres. It was quite a spectacle, Dobbie's giant head poking out the sunroof and three other dogs hanging out the windows, Freddie bellowing and getting the others to join him in the deafening chorus. Dobbie was fast. Sonny, with his long streamlined legs, ran like the wind. But Woozie, with much shorter legs, could stop him and bring him to his knees with her superior herding strategies. She kept them all in line.

Dobie rides with his head out the sunroof. Woozie peers through the window.

Except for Freddie, they all loved the beach, so we decided to rent a house at San Juan Capistrano for our vacation. Checking the newspaper ads for rentals, I chose the one that did not state "No Pets Allowed". All four dogs were piled into the Toyota with my housekeeper who would babysit them if we left. When I went into the real estate office to get the key, I saw the sign "No Pets Allowed." Well, there we were! What should I do, 'fess up that I have four dogs lurking in the car and turn around and go home? No, I decided to chance it and we moved into the beach house. (Are you beginning to wonder if I have an "authority" problem?) Oh, my. The dogs loved it. We kept a bucket of water and towels on the deck to clean off the sand. The house itself was "beach" quality. And dirty. It was a good thing we brought Mimi because she spent an entire day just cleaning the refrigerator. After a few days, the place looked neat and scrubbed. Jack went to a marine store and bought lengths of rope and made a fence to keep the dogs from jumping off the deck. One day Dobbie and I took a long stroll down the beach. We spotted, way in the distance, like a miniature, a huge dog, maybe a Great Dane. The dog saw us and took off in our direction. I told Dobbie, "Let's get out of here." He got the message and we ran like crazy to get to the safety of that roped-in deck, barely making it before the Great Dane attacked our flimsy fortress. Dobbie didn't retreat. He did what he could to defend his turf backed up by Woozie, Sonny and Freddie who lined up in the defense, thus repelling the invader. Such were the adventures of that week. But there were to be more. We were discovered! Woozie and Sonny go to the beach and are joined by a friendly dog.

Dobbie, who might not like another dog around has to stay home with Freddie, who doesn't like the beach anyway. We decided to go shopping at the marvelous mall in Laguna and left Mimi in charge of puppies. When we returned, she met us at the door, warning us that the owner was there and that when she came in the house, the puppies were on the sofa. She apparently went "crazy", and had not recovered during the time she impatiently waited for us to return. Her black-dyed hair was standing straight up on her head, her face distorted, her bulging eyes flashing with anger. She carried on at length how we had "defiled" her lovely home and all the damage dogs they had done.

Our efforts to point out how clean the house was and how wellmannered the dogs were to no avail. She insisted we had to go. Now! She threatened to have her six foot son throw us out! Then our week-end guests showed up. I don't remember who suggested a deposit to cover any damage but she seemed to agree that $200 would do it, no check, only cash. It was to be refunded if there was no damage from the dogs. Before we left, we had the real estate agent inspect the house for possible damage. After an inspection she agreed that no damage was done and we should get the deposit back. You know, of course, that we never did get it back. But that week was worth the extra $200.

However, you can believe I'd never try sneaking four dogs in where they weren't wanted again. In fact, they were all kept immaculately clean. Bathing was in a portable plastic pool on the patio, and the three big ones would line up, waiting their turn, each watching the procedure carefully. Freddie was washed in the kitchen sink with the other three now watching apprehensively to see what was happening to him. They were indeed a pack. And even if Freddie hated Dobbie, he was frequently found curled up, snuggling next to Dobbie in their garage "bedroom".

You can tell Freddie is contented when he sticks. out a little pink tongue.

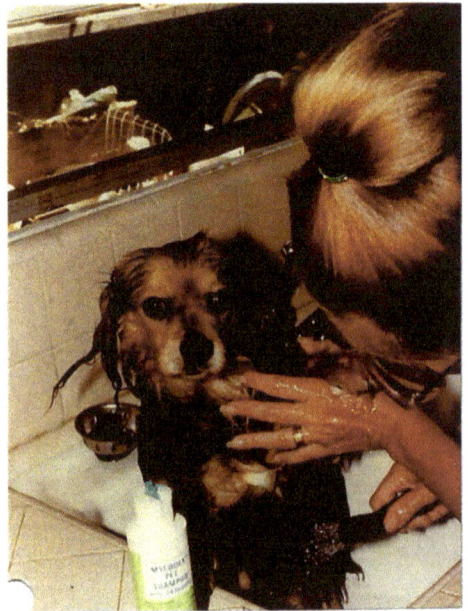

Freddie gets his bath in the kitchen sink.

Woozie played a kind of volleyball with us in the pool throwing it to her. She would hit it back with her snout. The game continued until the ball went out of bounds and Woozie got it. That was the end of the ball. It was great fun and entertained many guests. Dobbie wanted desperately to play, too, but couldn't figure out what the game was. But he wasn't to be underestimated. One time we saw rat run under the deck. All dogs took off after it. While they sniffed around, it escaped out the other side. I pointed in that direction. Dobie, now at one hundred and thirty pounds, was the only one fast enough to catch it. I watched with dismay as he carried it into the bedroom and put it on my bed. Well, he was *proud* of it.

Woozie plays volleyball in the pool hitting it back with her snout.

Woozie about to score a point.

Woozie "kills" the ball.

Puppies want to join Woozie in the game
if they can figure out what it is.

Sonny, being the underdog, was perhaps my favorite. As a puppy, I carried him around like a baby. The bond was so strong that sometimes, when I was out of town, I'd get a distinct kind of message from him. Some came with images.

Therapy Dog Bobo with his favorite toy.

Bobo at a mountain lake fetching a stick non-stop!

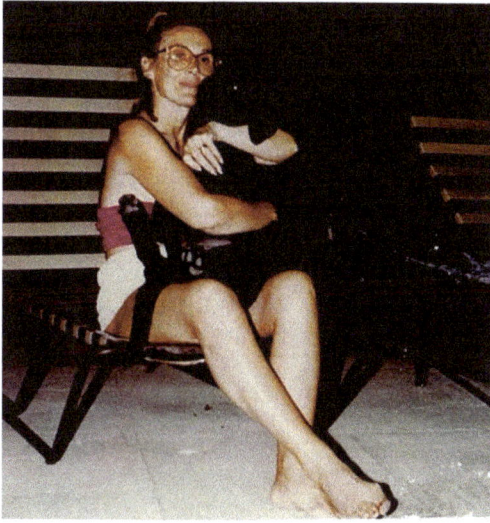

Sonny, the underdog, gets extra cuddling.

I felt sure he was trying to communicate with me. A lot of studies proved that they get messages from us—like five minutes before driving into the garage, a dog will move to wait by the door or watch out the window.

So it's not too much to think that the reverse could be true, that they could be trying to send us messages. They could be trapped in terrible frustration, trying to get through to us because we're not receptive. Anyway, he slept next to me. Dobbie slept in his basket until 6 A.M. every morning, when he would emerge, jump up on the bed, stretching out on my right side. Freddie slept curled up next to Jack's neck, Woozie by his feet. Fortunately, it was a king-size bed. It was menage Le Six!

We had seven years of unparalleled joy. Day after day was filled with fun, games and laughter, and then it began to quickly unwind. Dobie was the first to go with cancer of the spine. On the way to get that "final" shot, we stopped at Baskin Robbins and Dobbie has his last treat—a double dip ice cone. He gobbled it up enthusiastically Then Sonny with intestinal cancer. Finally Freddie with an incurable, paralyzing spinal disease. They were all cremated and buried in the garden they loved so much. At seventeen, Woozie was the last to go, the victim of strokes. All within eighteen months. It would be seven years before my heart was ready to take the risk of falling in love again.

Just one of the many happy days of Fun and playing with my four dogs.

Each has a special nickname: the Whoozie, Funny Freddie, Dopey Dobbie, and Sonny Sou Sou

CHAPTER NINE

A Mistake at the Shelter:
Starring *Beau Chien*, aka Bobo

Years later, now single and settled in a new community, with a new business, it was time to be enriched again with the kind of joy and love that comes with sharing your life with a dog. Christmas was a week away when I went to the Oxnard shelter to look for a small dog. Looking into to the cages, I saw a young black lab, very quiet, unresponsive, and the tears came. He reminded me of Sonny. But then I always cry at shelters, seeing those forlorn dogs mostly destined for extermination. The next cage had the cutest, little, fluffy mixed breed with lots of personality. He was my choice. I went in to close the deal only to be told that because it was just before Christmas, none of the dogs would be released until New Year's Eve. That was to prevent them from being used as gifts. Too many dogs had been given to people who were either unwilling or unable to care for them, ending up badly for the dogs.

When I went back on December 30, I saw my cute little, fluffy dog held by someone obviously taking him. Disappointed, I went into the shelter again. There was the black lab. The attendant said this would be his last day, his time was up. But he had no personality—no life. The attendant said, "Let's take him out in the yard" where he played and seemed normal. Reluctantly, I agreed to take him. On the way to the office, I passed the man who held my cute little fluffy dog. I stopped to tell him I had picked his dog out and had come today to get him. He said little fluffy dog wasn't really his—he had found him and brought him to the shelter. Knowing this would be his last day before extermination, he pulled him out to save him, but he still needed a home. Then he offered him to me, saying he believed I would provide a good home.

Thinking I had already made a commitment to black lab, I declined. But while standing in a long line, I ruminated. Here I go again. Trapping myself into something I really don't want to do. I want that little dog! Maybe I can have both of them. Don't be silly. You're lucky to take care of one now. But Black Lab is dull and Little Dog looks like so much fun. Now tearing up with indecision, I did what I believed was the right thing to do. I kept my commitment to Black Lab.

DOG!

NEVER BE LONELY

NEVER DESPAIR

SURE, LIFE IS UNFAIR

BUT YOU HAVE A FURRY FRIEND

WHO WILL LOVE YOU

TO THE END---

Printed in the USA
CPSIA information can be obtained
at www.ICGtesting.com
LVHW051749091223
766083LV00076B/2084